Lake Road 14:
Poems from Gardner Lake, Kansas

By Kiesa Kay

Cover photo, Gardner Lake Sunset, by Brian Schmiel
All other photos from the Henderson Family Collection

Dedication
To the Gardner Lake Cousins:
Diana, David, Terry, Carissa,
Jay, Paul, Shannon, Ki, DeeDee,
And most especially for
Larry Dean Webb

Table of Contents

Path Between the Peonies

Grandma liked to wear sandals
To show her pretty red pedicure
But every morning
When she stepped from the kitchen
To the swing beside the lake
Her feet got soaked in morning dew.
She carried socks in her pocket,
Grumbling a little as she sipped
Her cream-rich coffee.

Grandpa listened to her sputter.
He loved to watch her walk. He saw
How she meandered between the two
Peony bushes, then to the wild roses,
Past the grapevines.
One sunny afternoon, he poured
A concrete walkway,
Exactly matching the crooked path
Grandma stepped every morning.

Grandma kissed him.
They went to bed early.
Next day, she smiled all morning,
She filled up her pockets
With bread for the ducks.

Swinging Statues

First one cousin swings everybody
One by one as fast as possible
Till our feet fly up
Across the soft green grass
And we land splat kerplunk
And keep those positions

Then that cousin comes
And taps invisible buttons
So we have to act out something
Whoever wins
Gets to do the swinging
For the next round

Dee Dee won a lot
She could wiggle and giggle
And make her tummy wriggle
Plus she did the best cat noises

Mulberries

Diana, David, and DeeDee
liked the sweet ones best,
Dark purple and sticky
Lip-licking luscious
Staining fingertips

Me, I liked mine magenta,
Sour with pucker power,
So while the other kids
Ran wild, I'd slip up the tree
With my book under my t-shirt
Tucked into my shorts

I'd lean back on the biggest branch
Reading of fairies and knights
Till my own knight
Squeaker Reed
Brought his sack lunch to share
His mother packed
The best smooth peanut butter
With grape jelly on white bread,
Plus a banana or orange or chips.
He clambered up beside me.

Never, not once, ever
Did he say anything like
Bookworm or bluestocking
Or girls who read in trees
Turn into scraggly wenches.

Squeaker's parents
Taught him manners.
He gave me half his sandwich.
He split the chips evenly,
And I got the extra if the number
Went odd. He sectioned the orange,
Sharing the tiny baby pieces
That I loved best of all.

For dessert, we had mulberries,
A plentitude, an abundance,
Our purple picnic framed by the sky.

Gardner Lake Firefighters

Our guys couldn't afford a fire truck.
Instead, we had a fire Beetle –
An orange VW Beetle blazing red lights
On top. Mr. Reed, the fire chief,
Leaped into that Beetle to zoom
To the rescue, loud sirens blaring.
The hose sprung leaks and choked up.
Neighbors stood in bucket brigades
From the lake to houses on fire.
Once when the lake froze six inches deep,
The gals threw snowballs at the flames
While the bucket guys cracked the ice.
Once a house hadn't burned too much,
But the owner had no job and two kids.
Two guys snuck back after dark
And beat that porch splintered flat
Before the insurance adjuster got there.

Mud Puddle

Mud puddle, mud puddle
Round sticky glop
Put our bare feet into mud
Plop plop plop

Little froggy leaps away
Size of a small toe
Chasing on small muddy feet
To long prairie grass we go

Dandelions and clovers
Smash with scents so sweet
Slam jump back to mud puddle
Makes a walk complete

Early Spring Snake

Janie kicked her foot
Into a sleepy swimming snake
And it coiled up her leg
Circling her thighs

The echo of her scream
Splintered the air
And she kept kicking
Till the sleepy snake
Slid off her leg and into the lake

All us kids
Jumped in the murky water
Anyway – snakes or no snakes --
While one father
Watched us swim
BB gun at the ready
To shoot at slithering
Water moccasins

We didn't mind a bit
Next came tornados
And at last our favorite season:
Summertime

Playing House

Terry got called Duffy,
His toddler way to say Toughie,
Because Grandpa called him
One Tough Kid,
Ready to stand up
To protect all of us,
Come what may.

Duffy was little and cute.
When we played House,
We wanted him to be the Baby.
He said *No! Not cute! Duffy!*
He always wanted to be the Dad.
He'd take care of us, take care
Of everything, fix anything broken.
He'd sing, *Your man loves you, honey,*
Kind and strong and protective,
Just like Grandpa.

Mystery Date

Us girls never knew
Which guy we'd get.
Ki played Mystery Date for hours
With Karen at the Sanderosa
While all the other kids
Played outside in fresh air.
Karen wanted the fellow
With the tuxedo, all spiffy,
But Ki, she never got too choosy,
Short ones, tall ones,
Sporty, professional, overalls, suits,
Even the Dud date,
Dirty clothes and messy hair.

I want all of them,
She confided in Karen.
I want them all.

Mower

Dark night, new moon.
David took a long, heavy rope
To tie his dad's riding lawn mower
To the car's back bumper.

His buddy revved the car engine.
David hopped on the mower.
They zipped along backstreets,
Bouncing, popping, spinning.
The mower swung wide.
When his buddy mashed on the brakes,
David's ride went slamming sideways,
Into the ditch, overturning.
David leaped up,
Barely bruised,
howling with laughter.

The next day, his dad grumbled,
Dang, this thing can't stay in alignment.

Donkey Ears

All the kids rode the concrete donkey
From Mexico, with its cart
Full of bright flowers – daisies,
Chrysanthemums, zinnias.

One kid tore off its ears every time.
Who pulled off the donkey's ears?
Grandma stared sternly
Into every pair of eyes,
But nobody blinked back.

Grandpa knew who did it.
He took to keeping cement
At the ready,
Repairing those ears
Again and again,
Darting from the shed with cement
Before Grandma took notice.

Pillows

We all curled up in the living room,
Sipping hot cocoa under those paintings
Of Little Boy Blue and the Pink Lady.
The cuckoo clock sang the hour.

Diana fluffed up all the pillows.
Grandma had knit together washcloths
With strong yarn, and stuffed them
Full of cotton batting. We each got one.

Diana made sure everyone felt cozy,
Soft pillows, full cups, snacks ready.
She shared everything. She gave away
The softest pillows, and even traded back
Before the pillow fights.

Drive-In Movie

When Grandma wrapped
Chili dogs in waxed paper
With paper napkins, we got ready
For the good times.
We crammed into the backseat,
Four of us, with Grandma and Grandpa
Up front. The movies mattered
Not at all. Those chili dogs
Meant everything – tasty,
Paired with soda pop.

Sound crackled from a metal box
Propped on the rolled-down window.
If a movie got scary,
We covered up our eyes.
If a movie got mushy,
We giggled and groaned
Till Grandma hushed us.

We most always fell asleep
Before the second show.
Sometimes we woke up,
And by the light of the screen,
We saw Grandma and Grandpa
Holding hands, smiling in the dark.

Breitensteins

Family flung everywhere,
Fish fry in smashed potato chips.
We swim all day, out of the lake
Only long enough to grab more chips
We wrap in beach towels, dripping.
Michele's mom hollers
To put on some flip flops.
Beer tabs can cut small feet.
We catch crawdads by the claws
With ripped nylons stuffed with liver.
Then comes Marco Polo, holding breath,
Jumping off the concrete pier.
The sun sets. Night creeps up on us.
We catch fireflies by the dozens.
We trade wet swimsuits for dry pajamas.
Al plays his ukulele, singing,
Show me the way to go home.
Jesse says, *You're home already, Al.*
If you don't quiet down
These kids will be awake all night.

Square Dance

Stay on the quilt so nobody gets hurt.
Watch for those little fingers.

Grandma gave us her stern look.
We giggled, pulling hands back
From the edge of that quilt.

Grandpa tugged his bolo tie.
His shirt matched Grandma's skirt.
When we laid on our bellies,
Her fancy flat dancing shoes
Glinted gold at eye level,
Shining with rhinestone sparkle rainbows.

Allemande left with your left hand,
Right to your partner,
Right and left grand.
Get yourself around the ring.
Get to your partner, swing and swing.
Do si do your corner, do it right,
Then promenade your partner,
Your heart's delight.
Promenade.

Rainstorm

Streak lightning electrified the sky,
Followed by big booms of thunder.
We put on floppy red galoshes
Raincoats polka-dotted yellow pink green

Splashing into the front yard
We yelled as loud as thunder.
Mom placed pots and pans
Under all the ceiling drips pinging
Then gave us the pot lids
To clang and bang together.

Adrenalin fuels fright, fight, flight.
We found fun with fear in sight
Dancing with the raindrops.

Tornado

Ki watched the tornado
Swirling over the dam
Transfixed she stared
as the gray funnel came closer
The sky had turned olive green
In the middle of the day
And the air felt heavy
She heard her mother screaming
To get in the basement
The tornado didn't seem as scary
As that dank basement
Ripped from her perch
Pulled into the dark
She sank to her knees

Tornados smashed over the lake
Every May, sometimes several times
Into June and even April
Strangers died and rooftops tumbled
And one time the house next door
Landed in the front yard
Two walls and a floor intact
Even the outhouse ripped to splinters
The mulberry tree still standing

Three Pink Rosebuds

Diana, Dee Dee, and Ki
Became three pink rosebuds.
How delighted we were,
How delicately graceful,
Green netting for our skirts,
Like a soft spray of moss and leaves,
pink silk triangles, like petals,
With pink silky leotards
Encasing us, we stood
Straight and brave with shoulders back,
Perfect posture in first position.

We felt like princesses,
Pink princess rosebuds,
Turning, plies, pirouettes,
Our faces shining.

In dance class, we became
Three pure pink rosebuds --
Not yet in bloom, but ready.

Dancing Aunties

Aunt Jan and Aunt Linda
Loved *American Bandstand*
And *Soul Train*. We all danced
Before we could walk.
When we got bigger,
The aunties lined us up
In front of the couch to strut,
Do the Popcorn, twist and shout.

The more we danced, the happier
We got, and the more they'd give us
Sodas, chips, chocolate, and ice cream.

They told us to move with the music,
No need to watch our feet
Or each other – only feel the beat.
Spinning, soaring, sliding
We flew with feet on the ground
Freeing those dancing genes
Passed down – Ona Mae Ball,
Great-Grandma Jean, Eldeen,
And all the dancing aunties.

Firelight

Ice storm beyond knotty pine walls
Knocked all the lights out for miles
In sub-zero winter, wind howling.
Everybody gathered around
The only fireplace, heating lake water
To make coffee over the burning wood.
Grandpa danced in his long underwear.
Father danced in his dark red robe.
Us kids did scissors, paper, rock
To see who had to get the popcorn,
Going fast from beneath warm covers.
We cuddled close,
Each breath a cloud.

Then Grandpa passed gas – loudly.
Grandma squealed and smacked him.
He started to pull covers over her head.
She pinched her nose closed.
Kids, breathe through your mouths.
We giggled ourselves to sleep,
Snuggling and snickering.

Magic Refrigerator

Heat scorched the lake water from our
skin so we didn't need towels to dry,
But before we walked ten steps
We'd be dripping sweat anyway.

In sticky swelter of a hundred degrees,
Grandma's magic refrigerator offered
Ice cold soda pop, frozen candy bars,
Popsicles grape or berry or orange,
Fresh icy water, fudge-sicles,
Chocolate-dipped vanilla ice cream bars,
Green grapes, purple grapes, green olives,
Lemonade, limeade, kool-aid.

All us cousins trekked into the house,
Mouths opening like baby birds.
I don't know if I'm hungry or thirsty,
Dee Dee said, blue eyes gleaming.
Grandma grinned, saying, *Lemonade
made in the shade by an old maid.*
Us kids hollered, *You're not old,
Grandma,* and then we gulped and
slurped like greedy beaks till she said,
Mind your manners. Go outside and play.

Little Dipper

Orion's belt never beat anybody.
Shining brightly on new moon nights,
An arrow from his quiver
Pointed to the blinking star
Where we all began. Little Dipper,
Big Dipper, Cassiopeia –
We slept under the stars
From April to October,
Couch pillows beneath us,
Covered in thin blankets.
Low-voiced bullfrogs croaked
Our lullaby. Fish splashed deep.
A sweet honeysuckle breeze
Mingled with the constant clover
Or freshly mown grass.
Ten thousand twinkling stars
Swirled overhead, lighting our way
Home. We felt God resting up there,
Looking with love on the lake.

Feathers

In the morning, squawking
Awakened us. Snow white
Ducks and gray geese joined
Brown ladybirds and male mallards,
Feathers iridescent green and blue.
Quacking yellow fluff balls waddled
Land awkward but lake graceful.
They plopped one by one into the water.
White ducks had one grownup
To lead long lines of little ducklings.
Wild ducks traveled in twos,
Their little ones ranged between them.
With a great whoosh of feathers on wind,
Geese landed together. When they left
In V formation, the echo of their calls
Lingered long in the shimmering air.

Fireworks

Fourth of July meant family picnic:
Grandma's fried chicken, potato salad,
Eggs deviled with mustard,
Grilled hamburgers and hot dogs
With white buns, mustard, ketchup,
Iceberg lettuce, garden fresh tomatoes,
Grandpa's famous jello salad
With marshmallows and mandarins,
Beer for the men kept cold on the porch,
Soda pop, sweet tea, cherry pie, apple pie,
Chocolate cake with buttercream icing.

In daylight, Black Cat firecrackers,
Bottle rockets, smash ash snakes,
Swimming. At nightfall,
Flaring rocket tangles, Roman candles,
Fountains silver and gold and red
Against the black star-spangled sky.

One year after everyone went home
Sparks smoldered, scorched
Grandma's dock to cinders. Fireworks.

Sunset

Dusk sent sunset splashing
Pink frothing to bright orange darkening
Red with blue tinged purples erupting.
The sun slid to sleep behind the dam.
Day's last light glimmer rippled
As sparkles shimmied cross the lake.

Dee Dee whispered, *That sun*
goes to the other side of the world now
so folks there can feel morning.
Their day becomes our night.

We held hands,
Watching colors shift and change,
Imagining places we would travel,
Countries undiscovered,
Universes yet unseen.

34677340R00020